Echoes 11

Echoes 11

A Book of Poems

Ruth Stefano

To order additional copies of this book, contact:
Xlibris
1-800-455-039
www.Xlibris.com.au
Orders@Xlibris.com.au
790400

CONTENTS

FOR

MY DAUGHTER LIANA
MY SISTER MARGARETTA

SPECIAL THANKS

I give special thanks to my dear sister Margaretta for her support and encouragement, to my dear favourite and only daughter Liana for just being my daughter and last but by no means least to my printers and publishers Xlibris for causing this last dream of my life to come true – not forgetting all my dear friends for their greatly appreciated and ongoing support and encouragement, Thank you all so very much.

With love,

Ruth Stefano

INTRODUCTION

At the tender age of ninety, my dearest wish has been to publish my remaining poems before I depart this world, and so register my name on the list of published poets, thus avoiding my life's work disappearing in the mists of time.

My grandmother on my father's side wrote poetry so I guess I inherited from her this wonderful gift. Unfortunately, she didn't publish her work so when she died her poems died with her. Sadly, I didn't get the chance or opportunity to read any of her work. What a loss! So dear reader I trust you may enjoy the words of my heart, mind and soul – Happy reading!

THE ORCHID ADVENTURE

A thing of beauty is a joy forever
A famous poet was once heard to say
Thus I embarked on a brand new adventure
Marched blithely down the grand orchid way.

First there was one a soft fragrant one
With sepal and petal perfection
Then there were two, three four five and six
The start of my orchid collection.

Off then I went to my very first meeting
Amongst enthusiastic souls like my own
I took paper and pencil for pertinent jotting
Viewed species some members had grown.

I tried hard to look reasonably intelligent
Listened intently to each word that was said
But I have to admit in all honestly
Most procedures went clear over my head.

So I bought the odd book on the subject
Collected pamphlets and notes by the score
Determined to excel in my endeavours
Come out trumps as I'd oft done before.

I thought my education long since over
Wrong wrong it was only beginning
So I entered right into the spirit of things
Hell bent on the ultimate winning.

With 50,000 or so known varities
I took the whole baffling lot in my stride
Learning tribe names genus names and their species
And reciting them all off with great pride.

Cattleya epidendrum sophronitis
Cymbidium miltonia eulophia
Oncidium dendrobium phalaenopsis
Laelia odontoglossum and etcetera.

Well that left the collection fast gathering
And anticipation of seeing flowers sublime
But the years I learned most took in blooming
I'm afeared I'll sadly run out of time.

oooOooo

MODERN DAY POETRY

Poetry no longer belongs to the classics
Modern man has bended the age old rules
No longer sole ownership of the scholar
It belongs now to everyman academics or fools.

I wonder would Shakespeare turn in his grave
Keats Shelley Wordsworth turn pale
Would Robby burns cringe longfellow object
Seeing their modus operandi 'for sale'.

The bards of the ancients what of their view
Hearing rhythm and rhyme they held dear
Replaced with the doggerel by men of today
Scant attention to romance or tear.

What can one say its a sign of the times
Old values long lost gone forever
What can one do but quietly weep
Gone the beauty the sweetness endeavour.

But freedom of speech is a gift for all men
Regardless of interpretation
We write as we speak for the masses to hear
And in innocence create annihilation

Of all they held dear the poets of old
Of all they held holy in heart
Will they understand their spirits accept
That each age must bring a new start?

And perhaps all the poetry written today
Although styled simply and oft-times nonlyrical
Can be understood by those who may read
Thus making certain that all men are equal.

TO A SEDUCTRESS

Do you see her the wanton female
Look
Look at the length of her languorous limbs
Do you watch her the sly seductress
Have a care
She it is who watches you
Her smooth supple body lithe _
Lissome as liquid
Such a tantilizing teasing temptress is she
See how she moves
Slowly sensuously
Eyes focused on you
Her predictable her willing prey
Amber eyes
Hypnotic eyes weaving her spell
Daring you
Drawing you into the mystery of her space
Tauntingly exclusively magically hers
Ah she has you now
Surely securely - securely surely
Dazedly wondering what
What she is at
Soft now for she's the eternal queen
The inimitable
Cat.

ᴏᴏᴏ𝐎ᴏᴏᴏ

BEYOND PRETENCE

It's come the moment's come
The message drums a steady beat
And dazed awakening from a dream
I look about me - see at last
All the time honoured ploys props
Foibles gathered on the way
Knickknacks junk and say
What good are they
They only form a part
A background part of me
But I stay open naked to myself
No clothing ever could cover up
Nor truth the natural form disguise
Beyond pretence am I
All that lies buried in the past
Visual imagery static false
Now I am just me
I see me as I am
Stark reality
Open to my demons
My dark side my soul
My own real self
Therein lies true acceptance
Of me for me to me
My angels
To god.

oooOooo

A TIME TO WEEP

He was so beautiful
The young farm boy I saw today
Carrying his pails of warm foaming milk
Striding out across a lush green field
Fresh from the milking
Whistling a merry tune
Content in his labours
Happy with life
He woke in me such a feeling
Such a longing to go back
How far how far
Back to the time of sweetness
Back to the time of innocence
Before the time of inbetween
And so I in my watching wept
Wept with the melancholy of my thoughts
What have they done to us
Those who hold power over our existence
Stripped us of our rightful heritage
Our love and joy of simple things
And so I wept for you
For you and you - and me
And in my weeping
The voices of my mind asked
Who hears the acorn as it falls to kiss the earth
The music of water running with pebbles in a stream
The clear notes of a bird calling to its mate

The rustle of leaves tumbling in a playful wind
Where were all these sounds yesterday
In the years between
Have the birds been silent all these years
The winds still
Must we grow old to regain the time for hearing
For the mulling over and musing on things
Time to consider lost yesterdays
Time to weep?

oooOooo

I LOVE THE SUN

I love the sun
Not as a god or an idol or a shrine
But as a friend
Who brings comfort in a sometimes cold and
Cheerless clime.

I love the sun
It brings a smile to my lips and a warmth
To limb and bone
And as a friend
Helps to give me strength in the times
I feel most alone.

oooOooo

MOTHER DAUGHTER - THE ETERNAL LINK

Seed of my seed
Blood of my blood
Flesh of my flesh
Body of my body I bore her
Still she is not mine
I cannot claim her
Years I fed nurtured cherished her
Showed taught directed her
Watched her grow
Watched her slip away towards her own goals and
Understandings
Knowing ultimately knowing she was not mine
Her ears hear different whispers in the wind
Hear different songs in her heart
She sees with different eyes
Walks on different paths
So close yet parted by secret byways
Worlds apart with byways
She travels alone as do I
I do not really know her
She there - I here
Nor do I have control
How can one control a force of nature
It is so different
Always elusive
Ever changing

She is of me but never mine
And I knowing
We belong only to ourselves and to god
And so before I close my eyes in sleep at night
My last thoughts are always of her
My last words of prayer are for her
And when I wake at dawning
And tune in to earthly things
Birds stirring - sounds of nature
In my deepest depths of sadness
A tiny voice tells me be happy
Know yourself as truly blessed
Blessed for being chosen to bring this spirit
This individual this gift into this world
This world of opportunity and learning
And even tho' we hear the beat of different drums
Pursue our own directions
Even though I can never hold her
In the end all paths all rivers meet
Course on together as one unto the source
And the link - the link remains forever
Never broken
A bond into eternity and beyond
I her mother - she my daughter.

ooo○ooo

THOUGHTS

When I have things to do
I have not time to think
And that's good
To think for me is oft times sad
And brings me to the brink
Of maudlin mood.

Oh that thoughts could ever happy be
Unaware of place or time
And full of joy
The heart tuned in to sweetest song
The lilt of poets' rhyme
Of nectar cloy.

And that's the only thing
I think I'll do
A poet be
Thinking words of heart and head
Observing the rhythm of life
Poignant or happy.

What else is I ask myself
In the sure fast run of years
To be aware
And glancing store the mind
With passing picture parade
Is reality there?

Or is all this a dream
Perhaps the longest dream of time
Still a dream
Pathway to the real existence
Held fast in the soul's depth
Of rainbow stream?

I THINK

I think there is
No point in thinking too much
Or if one thinks about it
Seldom
Or even at all
Thinking is for scholars
Working out equations
Mathematical puzzles
Isosceles triangles and such ----
Philosophers
Pondering the perplexities of life
Why clouds ride the skies
The whys and wherefores of joy and pain
Thinking is for generals
Planning warfare strategies
Poring over maps
Instigating invasions-----
Financial advisors
Working out 'the dollar'
Get rich quickly schemes
Inventors dreaming up ideas for new gadgets or machinery----
Et cetera et cetera
Thinking is not for me
Who am I anyway
An insignificant mortal
One droplet in the ocean of life
A droplet that dissolves and blends with
The seething vastness of the populace

Not a thing that I think will change
The nature of things
Not in the grand picture
The overall plan
I could philosophize
Throw a few thoughts into the ring
However pertinent
However puny
For what?
For why?
The rain will fall
The sun will shine
Birth death and seasons
The inner struggle to understand the reasons
So stop
Stop stop now stop
Trust
Accept
And let it all flow on
Regardless!

oooOooo

HI HO SPARROWS

I thought the flock of sparrows
Atwittering in the tree
Had chosen my establishment
For living comft' ably
The noise they made each morning
And in the afternoon
Convinced me they had found a place
Their hearts were most in tune
Such merry little fellows
Hi ho hopping on the ground
Then trapezing up in foliage
With most contented sound
Oh happy winged creatures
Fulfilling every wish
Eating insects on the branches
Quenching thirst in my dog's dish
I watched the flock cavorting
From morning till near dark
And saw with some annoyance
Where they always left their mark
My deductions were misguided
This place of lodging not their 'bide'
Twas the crusts of bread and goodies
On the fence's other side
For there lived quacking ducklings
Tho' temporary still most able
Being fattened by their owners

To grace somebody's table
And nothing lasts forever
So surely came the day
The sparrows took flight elsewhere
When the ducks were whisked away.

AUTUMN

How I love the autumn
It's a quiet time
A time of quiet days
When the soft hush of the season fills the air
And the remnants of summer
Almost unnoticed
Finally slip away
It's a time of deep reflection
Unhurried contemplation
Relaxed observation of nature
Savouring of sights and sounds
Lizards basking in the autumn sun
Doves cooing in the distance
Birds playing lazy chase from tree to tree
It's a feeling of slowing down
Gathering together the last measure of warmth
Before the long hard days of winter set in
It's that time between heat and cold
When the heart and mind take stock
Happy to be a part of this gentle time of year
When one wants each day to last forever
Gone the heat, the urgencies, strains and tensions
Autumn is nature's relaxant to a troubled mind
A velvet glove to ease a tired body
When breezes caress
Content to play
And the sun warms the soul
This time is when god's message of peace and love
In all the silent spaces
Can be truly heard.

oooOooo

MATTHEW FLINDERS - MAN OF VISION

Imagine with what trepidation
Out of Sydney 'the Norfolk' set sail
Venturing into unchartered waters
Riding rough seas - battling a gale.

All hail to young Matthew flinders
A man of brave vision was he
Not knowing just what lay before him
Embarking on this uncertain journey.

The date July 16 1799
And Matthew no rank misgiver
His mission to charter a coastline
Seeking possible ports - map a river.

He took shelter in pumice stone passage
When 'the Norfolk' developed some leaks
All around him the lush Aussie bushland
In the distance our grand 'glasshouse' peaks.

He was awed with the splendor and colour
So diverse from the land of his birth
The unique wildlife birds trees flowers
A wondrous new land of great worth.

The natives he found mostly friendly
And he marvelled their culture and craft
Fashioning of fishing nets boomerangs hunting tools
Canoes and huts made from trees and tree bark.

While his men set to repairing 'the Norfolk'
He mapped out the shoreline - odd cove
What joy inspiration what feeling
Discovering Bribie's vast treasure trove.

He explored with excitement the area
Named numerous spots on the way
Woodypoint pumice stone river (passage)
Not forgetting our great Moreton bay.

Matthew was recognized as 'man of the moment'
On return to his own english town
And we folk that live here on Bribie
Give thanks for this man of renown.

He'll be part of our history forever
And with just cause we commemorate
Give praise to the foresight and daring
Of Matthew flinders - man of vision designate.

oooOooo

AN OBSERVATION BEHIND GLASS

It's a grey morning
A decidedly damp beginning to a day
With rain droplets hanging from greenery
Wet shadows on fences
Grotesque figurines
Gutters like miniature rivers
Coursing along roadsides
Water pooling and puddling in low areas
The snails are happy
Trundling their homes across wet grass and concrete
Slowly and steadily
Savouring the moisture
The birds are happy too
Joyfully splashing in instant baths
With meals out of hiding
What a feast time
Open sport
Only I have a sense of misery
I feel trapped
I can only look from the inside
Observe behind my prison of glass
The picture for me is grey
Damp and grey
Grey skies grey fences grey snails grey birds
A decidedly grey outlook
Then as a patch of blue appears
And the sun breaks through the clouds
There's an intermingling of colour

Flashes of firecracker light
Grey inverting to blue
Blue merging with drifts of white
White drifts floating
Floating in a sea of blue
A kaleidoscope of change and contrast
Deepening
Intensifying
Greenery becoming more green
Reds yellows more vibrant
Like fresh paint
Lovingly stroked by an artist's brush
Suddenly the scene
The day
Bursts into life
How wondrous is the hand of nature
And I the prisoner
The observer behind glass
Feel instantly free
Instantly happy.

oooOooo

BOATS

Boats lying at anchor
Are open to the whim of the sea
Riding the heave of the changing tides
Or submitting to calm peacefully
Becalmed and at rest peacefully.

Boats slave to king Neptune
Mighty monarch of water and wave
Bowing to his infinite power
Knowing naught from his rule can be saved
From his rule naught can be saved.

Boats dipping and bobbing
Pulling moorings in the merciless swell
Flung adrift by the rage of their master
Or beached to the sound of the knell
To the low mournful sound of the knell.

Boats casting ghost shadows
Silhouette against black of night sky
Or floating on shimmering waters
When the moon sheds her light from on high
Sheds her golden light from on high.

Boats quietly idling
Lie cradled in the arms of the sea
While they rest they recall the stories
Of tales they alone hold the key
Dark tales they alone hold the key.

Boats whispering murmering
Only ears of the chosen can hear
Longing to share all their secrets
With the listeners unafraid to draw near
Listeners not afraid to draw near.

Boats of seafaring passage
Waiting in sun in wind and in rain
Slave to king Neptune friend to man
They wait to sail out once again
Sail out on the sea once again.

oooOooo

PERPLEXITIES

Sometimes I look at the moon
As it smiles from its perch in the sky
And I wonder the reasons why
Tho' age old it appears so jejune.

Ofttimes I look at the sun
Even tho' it dazzles the eyes
And I feel I am not being wise
For this passtime I really should shun.

On occasion I study the stars
Now there lie some stories to tell
Exciting configurations as well
With 'unknown' among all the regulars.

Then of course I like viewing clouds
How differs the size colour shape
A constantly changing 'scape
The extraordinary scene thus endows.

What a puzzle I find in the sky
Alas I am only a mortal
And may never enter the portal
Of the secrets of life that ask why?

oooOooo

CHRISTMAS

The sights and sounds of Christmas
Are with us once again
Bells ringing
Choristers singing
Frosted scenes on window panes.

A million light bulbs fairy twinkling
Framing Santa and his sleigh
Smoothly gliding
Rooftop riding
Rudolph's nose to guide the way.

Christmas wreaths of pine and holly
Welcome plaques on neighbours door
Puddings making
Mince pies baking
Mulled wine warming set to pour.

Trees with baubles snow and tinsel
Glittering stars and angel wings
Parcels piling
Mysteries beguiling
Pressies ties with coloured strings.

Church doors open and inviting
Jesus story to ordain
People praying
Message saying
The Christmas spirit here again.

Hark the herald angels singing
Away in a manger little donkey in stall
Sweetest melling
Voices telling
The very first Christmas of all.

Prayers for brotherhood of nations
Hopes for worldly bond to reign
Friendship stealing
Loving feeling
Peace on earth goodwill to men.

oooOooo

THE TALE OF BILLY THE BUMBLER

They called him Billy the bumbler unswerving
A title I felt undeserving
I thought him true blue
But what could one do
When he bumbled through life quite unnerving.

He walked with the weight of world troubles
His poor brain was forever in fuddles
There was really no doubt
What e'er he was about
Brought catastrophes mostly in doubles.

Poor Billy was butt of much 'jokels'
Desperately wanting to pass all the focals
He tried hard to fit in
But he just couldn't win
So remained on the 'out' with the locals.

One day with a sniggering mutter
They set his poor heart in a flutter
Not really quite cricket
Gave him a tatts ticket
Found muddied and torn in a gutter.

You can imagine the all round guffawing
Watching Billie homebound spirits soaring
They could not give a jot
A despicable lot
Waiting Billie's downfall - so deploring!

Tho' simplicity being Billie's main motto
Next day 'round the bar voice 'unsotto'
Said 'it's drinks all aroun'
I'm a man of renown
I've just won first prize in tatts lotto!

The moral of this tale to some sadder
Respect the 'plebs' at the base of the ladder.

ᵒᵒᵒO ᵒᵒᵒ

SONNET TO A GALLANT KNIGHT

How fortunate the damsel of the olden day
True love and ardour hers alone to claim
With gallant knight to battle love's sweet name
His sword victorious at her honouring feet to lay.

In modern times the knight intent upon the sport
Thinks not to sacrifice his all and else for love
Determined but to fight his strength to prove
His glory and not for the lady the battle fought.

So this fair lady then with longing dream
Waits on with deepest faith and fervent prayer
Her princely knight's appearance from out where
Perchance to write 'fulfilment' over 'might have been'.

The pangs of unrequited love give rise to poetry
While weeping heart lies hidden from the sight of ecstasy.

SONNET TO A FEARFUL HEART

Ah no dear one not at your door would want my heart to lie
Unguarded unprotected from your feet to stomp and tread
And then despairing break, break and be as dead
While you unfeeling onwards walk and pass me by.

Ask not that I should love with scant regard to price
Such sacrifice too much this gentle heart to bear
Awaking not in you the willing want to cherish and to care
And careless toss aside the promised winning dice.

Too much too much - why never sees the open eye
And looking finds its complement with fairest grace
The mirrored acquiesence in another's glowing face
Heart reaching yet to heart in longing sigh.

Thus heart's feet afraid to take a chance
May never in love's rondelet begin to dance.

oooOooo

SONNET TO A LOVER

Line the clouds of my love with gold
Oh my lover
Line the clouds of my love with gold
Fill my dreams with wonders untold
Oh my lover
Fill my dreams with wonders untold.

In your silences hear my hearts yearning
My lover
In your silences hear my heart's yearning
Make sweet the songs of love's burning
My lover
Make sweet the songs of love's burning.

Stay the thrust of my piercing sorrows
Oh my lover
Stay the thrust of my piercing sorrows
Bring the promise of all your tomorrows
Oh my lover
Bring the promise of all your tomorrows.

Let our footsteps seek onward the path of love's wind
And the tendrils of love grow forever entwined.

oooOooo

IF I SHOULD

If I should die for love of you
Would you think more of me?
If I should swoon for wanting you
With heart in hand and seeking you
Beseeching pleading needing you
What then would your thoughts be?

If I should lay my love at your feet
Would you think more of me?
If I should live my life for you
Forsaking cherished dreams for you
Oblivious of none but you
What then would you think of me?

So the fire of love warmed by flames of desire
May leap to love's touch or grow cold and expire.

HEED NOT THE EAST WIND

Heed not baby mine to the promises of the east wind
He would try with all his might to draw thee from
Thy mother's knee
But not half so strong is his strength
As the strength of thy mother's love for thee

Watch not my little one his flowery gifts
He whisks the petals of the magnolia tree and scatters
Them at thy tiny feet
But not half so sweet is the fragrance
Of the magnolia petals as thy mother's love for thee is sweet

Feel not baby mine the coaxing of his caresses
He blows his breath to encircle thee with warmth
From above
But not half so warm is his warm breath
As the warmth for thee of thy mother's love

Listen not my little one to the murmer of his voice
He sings to thee with music soft and high
But not half so musical are his songs
As the lullabies of thy mother's love for thee ever nigh.

ooo◯ooo

CONTRASTS

The currawong calls in the distance
The radio plays in the fore
The sun streams its beams through the windows
The puppy dog yaps at the door.

The doves lazy coo in the arbour
The housewife kneads her bread dough
The wind blows the leaves in the treetops
The children play tag to and fro.

The magpies low murmuring warble
The police cars all sirens ablare
The lizards lie silently sunning
The speedboats fast race to the dare.

The mountains and valleys so tranquil
The city's loud noises and clang
The stream pebble running agurgle
The guyfawkes day fireworks bang.

Thus moves the eternal balance
Between mother nature and man
The scales somehow tipping at evens
Finding levels since earth's time began.

oooOooo

QUESTIONS & ANSWERS

Old woman old woman what are you thinking
Where do your thoughts run today
Your years have grown strong with your memories
Your body the price one must pay
Your face maps the pathes of your travels
What force then has guided your way?

My daughter I'll tell you my story
How I planted an oak long ago
In the garden of life was it planted
In the arms of the rich earth below
Each morning I studied its progress
And with interest I watched my tree grow.

Old woman old woman what are you dreaming
Where do your longings aspire
Do you dream of past visions and yearnings
Are you still adding fuel to your fire
Or are your ambitions fast quelling
And heaped on the bier of the pyre?

My daughter I've watched with acceptance
How life brings with it sorrow and pain
How the wind blows the leaves of the oak tree
How the sky sends its hail and its rain
How the birds wait resigned and in patience
Then rejoice with their songs once again.

Old woman oh why are you weeping
What is your reason for tears
What is it that causes you sadness
Gives vent to your doubts and your fears
What sorrow pulls so at your heartstrings
And darkens the light of your years?

Sweet daughter I weep for the children
For the innocent souls here on earth
Who are battered by life as my oak tree
Without love without hope since their birth
Who never will know their potential
Nor ever discover their worth.

Old woman say then why you're smiling
What secrets of life can be told
How serene how at peace your demeanour
As the oak tree what strengths you enfold
What message of faith can you give me
What promise of hope to behold?

Ah daughter my reasons for smiling
The years of observance do prove
That all things grow sturdy and strongly
When nurtured with help from above
With sun and with rain and with patience
With wisdom and enduring love.

oooOooo

THOUGHTS ON A DEAD MAGPIE

He lay there dead
A magpie
Under the spread of a tall eucalypt
Probably his home
His wings spread out
Head turned upwards
As if to catch one last glimpse of sky
His sky
How silent now
No joyous warble
No freedom flights of soaring up into the blue
Dive bombing down
No exchange of song
Chatter with neighbour birds
Was this the end of his existence
This hush
This silent nothing
Where will he go
Will his soul take flight to bird heaven
To fly again
To meet with friends
To reminisce on earthly things
Adventures feasts
Family chores and fun
Or will this once proud bird in lonely death
Merge slowly with the ground he lies on
A dying twig from his beloved tree
In mournful sympathy beside him.

ooo O ooo

MUSINGS ON A FALLEN ROSE

The rose is fallen
Two long weeks it strove
Lavishly sharing itself and its perfume
Giving joy to the beholder
Giving nectar to the bees
Broken finally
Fragmented
Spilled out --------------
Of beauty born
And still of beauty died
Faded and overblown
I had watched from when it budded
With strength and grace
Pressed its petals out proudly
Anxiously to life
Regal and stately in all its full glory
Now bedecked with crystal rain droplets
Now crowned with diadems of dew
Now perfect
Satin smooth as doeskin velvet
Oh gracious rose
Indeed the fairest queen
Among all flowers.

oooOooo

THOUGHTS ON OUR QUEENSLAND

This fair, this lush, this golden state
With Queensland as its name
Who could deny its 'welcome' feel
Deserved in its fame.

How green its blend of palm and tree
How colourful its flowers
How sweet its birdsong trilling forth
From hidden nests and bowers.

The blue of skies of endless seas
The sparkling waves and sands
Who could resist the magic lure
Gateway from other lands.

What rare delight those luscious fruits
Such tempting palate pleasers
The fish, the prawns, the 'moreton bugs'
'To kill for' tasty teasers.

Warm evenings spent beneath the stars
With moonlight's silvery glow
The happy beam of friendship's smile
Best Aussie state I know.

oooOooo

"A TRITE SAYING"

There's a saying that's trite
But it's certainly true
'Do unto others as you'd have them do to you'
This gives pause for some thought
As you have to admit
And also great scope as of course will befit.

Let us study this carefully
And try hard to accrue
How this may benefit others and may benefit you
On the other hand plainly it could cause so much strife
Giving rise to dilemmas that may last all one's life.

So wisely I feel 'twould be well to desist
From the doing, thus we should resist
To play a safe game would seem better by far
So that others and you can move on without spar.

oooOooo

A SEDENTARY LIFE

A sedentary life is soothing
A sedentary life is smart
A sedentary life is smooth
And warms the cockles of your heart
But let me give a warning
Don't foolishly get caught
The price of giving in to bliss
A sedentary life is short.

END OF DREAMTIME

She sat at the door of her humpy
Cradling her head in her hands
And idly while focusing memory
Scribed shapes with her toes in the sands.

The pictures passed slowly before her
The hunting grounds she knew as a child
When the whole land belonged to her people
Who roamed free o'er this vast domicile.

When they ran with the dingo and emu
When they swam with the dugong and cray
When they hunted with boomerang and spear stick
Dug for yams in the cool of the day.

They knew all the burrows and water holes
Where best game and best fish could be found
Where the wild berries ripened in season
Where the crocodile eggs slept underground.

How she loved all the tales of the Dreamtime
Told by elders 'round campfires at night
All the rituals, songs, tribal dances
Thru' the ages her peoples' delight.

As she dwelt on her pictures of memory
A slow tear coursed its way down her face
And she sighed with a deep heartfelt knowing
Time could never go back for her race.

All those days of the Dreamtime were over
Their way of life in the great wilderness
This is what white man called progress
This loss of their very uniqueness

Yes their stories were bound up in volumes
In schools as history read and taught
A sad end to a proud peoples' culture
But a remnant – let no man disport.

So this was the close of an era
All her tribe had held sacred long years
Devoid of the magic of Dreamtime
And replaced with but memories and tears.

oooOooo

THE 9.34

The train was departing at 9.34
And oh what a sense of elation
She had somehow survived
The day'd finally arrived
She was here at long last at the station.

She had waited forever or so it seemed
For this momentous trip to unravel
Born and bred on the land
She was but a new hand
At this modern day method of travel.

When one's lived all one's life in the country
Far away from the big city battle
Feet, cycle or horse
Were one's only recourse
To get round about folks, land and cattle.

The decision was made – adventures to be had
And who knew what great things were in store
The die had been cast
She'd found freedom at last
The train was departing at 9.34.

Long years had her dreams been to wander
To explore 'greener' pastures elsewhere
Her need was to prove
That this land that she loved
Was the closest to heaven by far.

She checked for the time on her wristwatch
As she boarded and closed tight the door
Joy and wonder within
Let the journey begin
The train was departing at 9.34.

THE MULLET FESTIVAL

Well its that time of year on our Bribie
When the locals get into the fray
Even tourists jump into the action
Make the most of a 'mullety' day.

It's the Apex Club's Mullet Festival
And it's held at this time of each year
Raising money for rendering assistance
To needy groups or individuals out there.

There's all sorts of great entertainment
With floats and a Festival Queen
Lots of stalls, rides and yummy food outlets
Entertainers and fireworks to be seen.

There's the local Girl Guides grand Duck Derby
And the major event of the day
That 'not to be missed' 'Mullet' throwing
God help those who may get in the way.

It's all about who throws the furthest
From holding that fish in its place
To tossing it out in the distance
Without sploshing someone in the face.

It's just mayhem with screams shouts and giggles
And the poor fish all twisting in fear
For sure quit their seasonal 'running'
To a more disposed time of the year.

ooo〇ooo

XMAS THOUGHTS DOWN UNDER

The kangaroos are jumping
Their tails on red earth thumping
And galahs in leafy treetops chattering free
The brolgas all are dancing
And emus too are prancing
Excitements building everywhere to see.
It's Xmastime again down under
The vibes are all around
Of ringing bells of carousels
Of every joyous sound
The parrots and the lorikeets
All bright with Xmas hues
Are screeching out the happy song
The yearly Xmas news
Wild ducks on ponds are skimming
Soft hum of buzzing bees
It's all bliss and tranquility
Out back 'mongst tall gumtrees
And in our suburb dwellings
It's time for contemplation
Time to give thanks to our God
Time for blessed celebration
To ask what Xmas means to us
It means so many things
The holly pine and mistletoe
The peace that yuletide brings
The sounds of church bells ringing
Hand held candles flickering weave

'Tween voices carol singing
On a Holy Xmas Eve
And then on Xmas morning
It's such a joy to see
The glow on little faces
Finding presents 'neath the 'tree
It means togetherness in families
Cards sent to friends held dear
Old friends and also new ones
Had live both far and near
It means prayers of supplication
To hear again the story
Baby Jesus in a manger born
The witnesses to glory
It matters not how young how old
This time's with one accord
Rejoice and with united voice
Give love and praises to our Lord

WITH WHAT TO DO

So now as one door closes tight behind
And the glimmer of a new door lies ahead
I find my footsteps tread an unfamiliar
Path

Wind through secret forests of my mind
Untouched and unexplored – with what to do
Freeze immobile as the wife of Lot
Gaze with unbearable longing on your
Horizon face

Be bound in chains of my forbidden truth
Or listen to the sweetest music of my heart
Bridge the span of mind – overlook delusion
Slip the cloak of false naïve timidity

Open the Pandora Box of my deepest desires
Reach out my hand to you in trust and faith
And wait in patience sweet – dear love willt take it?

ooo O ooo

OUR OUTBACK AUSTRALIA

Oh it's a dry land a brown land
As stark as ever seen
But very now and then one sees
A little patch of green.

The gnarled old gums once proud and tall
Windswept and sideways lean
Still brave new leaves contribute to
A little patch of green.

A parched land a barren land
With skies of azurine
And here and there in red gold earth
A little patch of green.

Out there 'midst scrub and granite rocks
Old hills sagely serene
Stand guard o'er quiet valleys
And each little patch of green.

No oasis in this desert land
No relief the eyes can glean
A seared scarred land with here and there
A little patch of green.

But it's our land our outback land
What matters where we've been
Hearts leap our sunburnt land to see
And each little patch of green.

ooo𝐎ooo

A DOZY OBSERVATION

Queenslanders in summer don't go to their beds
When the temperature's up and they've got
fevered heads
When the air is so thick
You could knock with a stick
Then I've noticed that Queenslanders don't go to
their beds
(or so it would seem)

You may ask how I know and the answer's
right there
When I give up the fight and I totter downstairs
I can see with surprise
Thru' my sleep deprived eyes
Scores of house lights atwinkling around everywhere
(and I know it's no dream)

So what they all do you may well ask of me
To which question I can but reply personally
I just wander about
Half zonked in and half out
As for t'others I'm darned if I know – you tell me
(things are not what they seem)

oooOooo

JOHANN SEBASTIAN

When you and I were young my friend
The skies were always blue
The choices all were ours my friend
So many things to do.

The roads were wide and long my friend
No stumbling stones in sight
And we were full of dreams my friend
The future new and bright.

The whole wide world was ours my friend
Our star was rising high
And God smiled down on us my friend
From a rosy blushing sky.

I could not e'er forget my friend
That first soft breathless kiss
When lips sought lips and found my friend
Such all consuming bliss.

Those were the learning days my friend
When bloods were running strong
The gift of time was sweet my friend
And all of life a song.

Our melodies we sang my friend
With aspirations high
What happened to those days my friend
That went so swiftly by?

They say that love is blind my friend
Minds blocked 'gainst differing factions
We reap what e'er we sow my friend
Consequences of our actions.

So what do we see now my friend
Now time is almost done
With choices long gone by my friend
And days all but outrun?

We took such alternate roads my friend
And distanced each the other
What lessons did you learn my friend
When we were not together?

So now we're old and grey my friend
Reminiscing on the past
Perchance we'll meet again my friend
Spend long sweet time at last.

oooOooo

AN OLD FASHIONED TALE/TAIL

His walking stick was solid wood hickory
It stood proudly by the Grandfather clock
And tho' housed with the dazzling umbrellas
One could see 'twas superior stock.

It had been handed down o'er the ages
Surviving years of consistent good use
It was old it was gnarled it was pitted
And had weathered all forms of abuse.

Now this walking stick had quite a story
Which only close family were told
How it came into HONOURED existence
Carefully listen and the tale I'll unfold

The stick was honed by great grandpappy
Who felt every home should be armed
And the clock part of great ma's wedding Dowry
To be used as a reliable alarm.

So, long ago before present suburbia
When the forefathers lived in rough Barns
'Mongst the rugged terrain of the
country And the creatures that shared their small farms.

In winter when snow covered the landscape
And the cold winds froze whiskers & paws
The smallest of fur coated rodents
Sought comfort in the warmth of indoors.

One evening as great pa got settled
in his chair near the grandfather clock
A mouse brushed on past his recliner
And gave poor great grandpa a shock.

But as fast as old speedy Gonzales
He grabbed out at his hickory stick
And flayed all about at the culprit
Who got out of his way lightning quick.

It ran up the leg of pa's trousers
Then jumped to the face of the clock
Then somehow got caught in the workings
'cos the clock started wheezing dick dock.

Great pa was but seconds behind him
As the clock grinded in to strike one
Pa let out a great fiendish screaming
Yelled 'gotcha' as the stick found its home.

'twas the clock 'cos the rodent ran onwards
Towards the safety of his snug family nest
Whilst great pa slumped down in his armchair
And viewed all the debris he'd left.

The clock 'tweren't the same from then onwards -
It coughed, gurgled and wheezed all the while -
But the stick is still serving its purpose –
And the mice hold their own by a mile.

ooo**O**ooo

DOGGIE DOINGS

(DELIGHTS & DILEMMAS)

LEXI

Can you hear me Lexi darling
If I call to you out loud
Are you up there gently resting
With your dear head on a cloud?
Can you hear the angels singing
As they welcome you back home
So so happy you've returned to them
You only were on loan
As for me my heart feels broken
My dearest sweetest little friend
That the time you spent beside me
Needed finally to end.
So much joy your presence gave me
For this oh so short a while
Even thru' the world's worst troubles
Somehow you caused my heart to smile.
'twas you taught me many factors
How to rise above the pain
How to rise above each problem
Bravely face the world again.
I shall miss you little sweetheart
Weeps my heart with sad despair
But I feel deep down inside me
You will surely reappear
While you sleep my precious Lexi
Memories will hold me fast
Trumpets herald our awakening
Eternal Paradise at last.

oooOooo

TO BE OR NOT TO BE - SICK
(from a dog's point of view)

Something's wrong with my mum's voice
It seems to come and go
And when she tries to say something
It comes out cracked and low.

She's also looking rather pale
With not the usual fire
And when she bends to pat my head
I sense things rather dire.

The effort seems to cause a bout
Of tickling nose, I fear
And sure enough when she gets close
She sneezes in my ear.

That forceful blast throws me afar
Which really worries me
I'd hate to be in parts unknown
When I get called for tea.

It saddens me to see my mum
In such a sneezy haze
I can't think why she'd make this choice
Of how to spend her days.

She's sniffing, sneezing, coughing, wheezing,
Stark anguish in her heart
And holding on to both her sides
In case she falls apart.

I cant begin to understand
What makes these humans tick
Their contradictory way of life
Is why they're always sick.

Why cant they be content like us
To sleep and play and eat
Let someone else look after them
That's what makes life real neat - 'easy'.

ooo𝗢ooo

THE RAINCOAT
(A Zuki Poem)

Oh mercy me my mother dear
Of my life is the bane
She's bought for me a waterproof
To help keep off the rain.

I wish she would consult me
Before taking such a plunge
She'd miss the nomination
Of vying for world's prize scunge.

How could she be so thoughtless
My small body to confine
I'm accustomed to my freedom
Not meant to toe the line.

It hampers all my action
Tied into this here rug
And only serves to give me
A claustrophobic bug.

When first she made me wear it
I plain refused to move
I couldn't understand just what
My mother tried to prove.

Of course I was determined
To shake the horror off
Till all the vibes quite clearly showed
My mum had had enough.

She really lost her patience
At my so stubborn streak
And when I still refused to budge
She gave my lead a tweak.

And then she walked me up and down
With loud and pointed sigh
I'll admit although it teamed with rain
I did keep snug and dry.

And grudgingly I have to say
This truth I cant refute
My raincoat is a stunning hue
And I do look kind of cute.

IT'S A DOGS' WORLD

Well dogs have really come into their own
If you asked them they'd say it's high time
From the subservient mut to the glittering star
From the ridiculous to the sublime.

You can see them around wherever you go
Primping and posing and having a ball
There is no mistaking the outgoing trend
They're all out there answering the call.

I'm inclined to place blame on the peerage of old
Jewell bedecked upper classes who led them astray
All that pampering lounging on royal knees
A matter of time to come into their 'day'.

Of course hollywood opened the doorway to fame
With the appearance of lassie rin tin tin and white fang
Benjie and that slobbering canine whose name I forget
101 dalmations who rushed in with a bang.

We have wonderful guide dogs as everyone knows
Police and rescue dogs oblivious of danger
Just lately there's been that great daewoo dog
And clever pookie filling scent bottles with 'amber.'

Yes they're used in those ads as seen on t.v.
Groomed for leading parts in movies as well
They're posing for pinups and odd toothbrush ads
And any other darn thing that might sell.

What about the latest in high fashion modes
Vests, caps, cute shades for the eyes
Boots to avoid precious feet getting wet
Raincoats and mufflers for overcast skies.

It's an absolute must for hair crimping and makeovers
Manicures and pedicures with the podiatrist
And if the fast lane gets your pooch all stressed out
It's appointments with the local psychiatrist.

If you chance to go by your favourite book store
It's not bluff nor either some ploy
The latest best seller is there right on the shelf
Especially for dogs chinese feng shui.

And books on dog heraldry are proudly displayed
Each breed has its own coat of arms
The new trick is tracing your dog's family line
Next thing they'll be reading dogs' palms.

There's no denying the destiny of man's best friend
Gone the happy hours spent munching a bone
They're out there earning their daily bread
While the smug owners are relaxing at home.

These canines are really bringing in the big bucks
One has to admit they're nobody's fool
I'm tempted to educate my own little dog
Way to go - I'll enrol her in school.

oooOooo

A DIET DILEMMA
(A Zuri Poem.)

My mother says I'm getting fat
I'm not sure what she'll do
I'm feared I've got lean times ahead
My intake cut in two.

I know by now that steely look
And that determined jaw
And 'cos she's bigger far than i
Her rule's eternal law.

My future looks a little bleak
I worry the duration
Of missing tidbits luscious treats
Of facing sure starvation.

No more porridge in the mornings
When winter takes a hold
No warm salacious honey milk
To help keep out the cold.

Oh gosh what else will disappear
My toast with vegemite
And probably all those fancy chips
Pre-dinner snacks at night.

Those moorish shortbread bikkies
To munch at arvo tea
Another treat crossed off the list
To fade in memory.

To be consigned to basic food
Just meant for dogs alone
With boredom only eased somewhat
By daily chicken bone

Wont do for this superior dog
This royal regal pup
The ancestors would turn in graves
To see this lowly sup.

I might as well lay down and die
With all this diet stuff
Must think of something i can do
To try and call her bluff.

I'll stretch right out upon the mat
So I look long and thin
I'll gaze at her with soulful eyes
So I will surely win.

I'll cry and whimper just a bit
And sag upon the floor
That's bound to melt her icy heart
It's always worked before.

Then if I lick my empty bowl
And seem I'm in some pain
She'll pity this beguiling pup
And feed me up again.

oooOooo

THE DHURRIE RUG

I'm not quite sure what's going on
But I think I'm in disgrace
My little mum looks mighty grim
The smile's wiped off her face
She only wears that kind of look
When she's got some sort of bug
And I somehow think it may concern
Her favourite Dhurrie rug.

I really don't know why the fuss
I'm sure she bought it on the cheap
It's only just the cast off coat
From some old Indian sheep
I mean we dogs are connoisseurs
A trait that's been inbuilt
So that's the reason I'm not feeling
Any mammoth guilt.

I'll bet that wooly native sheep
Was definitely low class
From some unknown nomadic tribe
Along the Khyber Pass
Or even worse part of a flock
Of rugged mountain climbers
Those rough and ready peasant types
Found 'round the Himalayas.

A pup like me – a thoroughbred
Ancestry long assured
Deserves at least a persian rug
Or one of like accord
I must admit I get put out
When I'm just not being noticed
So feel the need for drastic steps
As a formal type of protest.

I did try hard to catch her eye
To dutifully warn her
But when she kept ignoring me
I chewed right through one corner
That's when the sparks began to fly
My mother lost her temper
She carried on as if she had
Some human type distemper.

Well what's an active pup to do
When mother's just not there
Not paying heed to me at all
Too much for one to bear
I think it's time she sorted out
Some facts inside her mind
Accept I come from royal stock
With bearing hard to find.

Being petted pampered waited on
Is my deserving lot
But sometimes it just seems as if
She couldn't care a jot
She's giving me that look again
With "watch it Zuki" eyes
That intimate I'd best take care
Retreat with grace seems wise.

Oh well, guess life's not all that bad
Snug on a rug by a cosy fire
I'll dream this Dhurrie's gold spun fleece
My heritage aspire
Maybe I should play this by ear
Back down a bit – oh drat
Else I'll finish in the pits outside
On the prickly coir mat.

Cold reason prompts the age old guise
Diplomacy aplomb
For after all I know what side
My bread is buttered on
So mother dear put back that smile
Don't give your vent to "curry"
This wise young pup will settle for
One slightly chewed-up Dhurrie.

ooo**O**ooo

THE DEMISE OF THE DHURRIE RUG

Well guess that's it my favourite rug
My dhurrie's gone to god
This time it's had the well known "gong"
Been buried 'neath the sod.

What part was left of it of course
It's pattern somewhat changed
The shreds of jigsaw puzzle wool
Quite sadly rearranged.

This culprit dog - this regal pup
Brought up to bear all boredom
Gave in to low and basic traits
Succumbed to rebel wardom.

Oh horror pain and deep disgust
I thought my priceless treasure
Beneath such base degrading stuff
Not stoop to such a measure.

But temper won the upperhand
What seemed playful interaction
A peaceful game of twist and toss
Turned into altercation.

When then the stricken dhurrie rug
Lay limply on the floor
Our brave pup tried to drag her foe
Clean through the doggy door.

That's how I found the sorry mess
The victor left no doubt
The loser jammed in halfway land
Not in nor either out.

All efforts to revive the rug
Proved sorrowfully hopeless
The dhurrie giving one last flap
Became silently croakless.

That poor and unsuspecting sheep
Who gave her coat as friend
Could not have dreamt her gift to man
Would meet with such an end.

Which brought to mind the last ordeal
Dismissed as one-off transgress
In truth was to our gallant dog
Temporary unfinished business.

Our scheming pup did bide her time
'till the dhurrie lay defenceless
Then pouncing let frustrations out
And thrashed her victim senseless.

The burial with song and prayer
Had neighbours all agog
The rug now rests in god's good care
Please - does anyone want a dog?

ooo**O**ooo

WHERE IS SHE?
(A Zuki Poem)
(For Zuki)

She keeps on disappearing
I'm getting quite fed up
It's all so disconcerting
To this bewildered pup.

One moment she is with me
The next thing she's not here
I'm trying hard to be tuned in
And train my puppy ear

To pinpoint sounds around me
And get to know what's what
Who's coming and who's going
And who is on the spot.

It's so downright confusing
I think she's tricking me
She's diverting my attention
With wicked perfidy.

There's just so many doorways
My gosh it is a bother
I keep my eye on one door
And she goes out of another.

She creeps around like Moses
So I don't know where she's at
And never seems to be there
When I really need a pat.

Just when I feel abandoned
And cry a little tear
Some other door will open
And she will reappear.

One day I'll be so clever
I'll be the smartest pup
I'll know just what she's up to
'cos then I'll be grown up.

oooＯooo

LILLI

My name is Lilli and some think I'm a dog,
But I'm really a person you see,
'cos I sit at the table each morning
Up there on my dear mother's knee,
And I eat the same breakfast as they do,
Being hot buttered toast and milk tea.

Sometimes I get to drink coffee
From a saucer of course not a cup,
I have my own special blue one
That holds just enough for my 'sup',
And my father feeds me plain cracker biscuits
When I'm good and I've lapped it all up.

After breakfast is over it's housework
And I do a fast tour of the scene,
I check first the bathrooms and bedrooms
And note what is needed to clean,
I can tell at a glance whose the culprit
And where each of my parents has been.

I walk up and down in the passage
Very primly with my head in the air,
Just letting them know not too subtely
Making sure they're completely aware
I'm accustomed to first class surroundings
And my house must be tidied with care.

When I've supervised all of the house chores
It's time for my walk in the park,
I always get very excited
And hurry them up with a 'bark',
And I jump up and down which means 'hurry'
'cos I'm anxious for sport and a lark.

But first there's the matter of grooming
And out come the combs and the brush,
My father looks after my bathing
And it's not ever done in a rush,
He uses the best soaps and perfumes
When I'm finished I smell sweet fit to blush.

Then I walk in the park very proudly
And we start off relaxed and quite calm,
'til I challenge some other large 'person'
Which seems to create some alarm,
And I find myself scooped off the pavement
And held tightly in my mother's arm.

Of course I could handle the situation
I'm not afraid - not a whit,
It's only my parents who worry
And seem to be having a fit,
I wish that they'd just let me show them
I'm not nervous - well maybe a bit.

Home to lunch and I have to tell you
That cooking's my mother's delight,
But I must admit chicken's my favourite
And I gulf it down bite after bite,
Like my mother I keep right on munching
'til my tummy feels bloated and tight.

Then it's off for the rounds of the garden,
I give it one turn - maybe two,
Then I fall in a heap in the middle
And pretend I'm admiring the view
While I gather myself all together
And think what's the next thing to do.

Sometimes there's a carload of visitors
Who stop by my parents to see,
And I really lap up the attention
Oh they make such a fuss over me,
And my mother whips up the fresh scones
So I get to eat devonshire tea. (whew!) (groan!)

Then I might pose for a photo
That's after my afternoon rest,
I'm really an excellent model
And go into my posing with zest,
I'm quite the envy of all other persons
Who aren't so photogenically blessed.

There's pictures of me just all over
In albums and of course on the wall,
There's even one studio photo
That's proudly displayed in the hall,
I must be the most photographed person
And I reckon I'm missing my call.

Then it's dinner - oh oh my poor tummy
Feels by that time a bit of a bog,
Then I case the back garden for prowlers
And valiantly tramp thro' my 'fog',
Finally exhausted I collapse on my little bed, (where's the enos?)
So ends a day in the life of a ----------------
Lilli!

oooOooo

AN EPITAPH TO LILLIE

The sweetest sweetest little dog
There never could be found
She sleeps now deep and peacefully
Beneath the soft cool ground.

How many years of pure delight
We held her to our hearts
But comes the time oh saddest time
Our smallest gift departs.

And ever will her memory
Lie deep within the mind
Her dear precocious qualities
No sweeter doggie find.

Sleep sleep our dearest Lilli
That apple forehead kissed
Sleep sleep our bravest puppie dog
So sorely to be missed.

TO BE OR NOT TO BE - SICK
(from a dog's point of view)

Something's wrong with my mum's voice
It seems to come and go
And when she tries to say something
It comes out cracked and low.

She's also looking rather pale
With not the usual fire
And when she bends to pat my head
I sense things rather dire.

The effort seems to cause a bout
Of tickling nose, I fear
And sure enough when she gets close
She sneezes in my ear.

That forceful blast throws me afar
Which really worries me
I'd hate to be in parts unknown
When I get called for tea.

It saddens me to see my mum
In such a sneezy haze
I can't think why she'd make this choice
Of how to spend her days.

She's sniffing, sneezing, coughing, wheezing,
Stark anguish in her heart
And holding on to both her sides
In case she falls apart.

I cant begin to understand
What makes these humans tick
Their contradictory way of life
Is why they're always sick.

Why cant they be content like us
To sleep and play and eat
Let someone else look after them
That's what makes life real neat - 'easy'.

oooOooo

ZUKI

It seems like only yesterday she came into my life
A tiny furry bundle in a cage
And the love we found together as the years flew swiftly passed
Will ever be engraved on my heart's page.

Her endearing little body, sweet face, proud plumed tale
The loyalty and trust she gave to me
The unconditional love that never faulted never failed
She was my own sweet puppy 'Bon Ami'.

My precious little Zuki – she brought me so much joy
She gave to me a reason to be glad
Her limpid soulfull eyes could always speak to me with love
And help me through those times of bad or sad.

I will hear her soft paws walking on the footpaths of my mind
For as long as I remain on earthly land
And see her sweet form moving thru' the mists she's left behind
Trying hard deep down inside to understand.

Thru' my tears and core wrench reason I know she was on loan
And I thank God, when I see beyond the dark
I pray that in the final scheme when I too go back 'home'
My Zuki greets me with her joyous bark.

oooOooo

"NED"

Introducing my iron dog Neddy
Bought in Melbourne on a visit last year
A descendant of course of the "Kellys"
Historically still held most dear.

The family's well known where he comes from
And it's inbred for this dog to stay mute
His forefathers all trained by the Kellys
To watch over any ill gotten loot.

He stands guard by my patio doorway
Staunch as any iron dog could be
Never questions the wind or the weather
Just nods his tin head faithfully.

He does cause a small worry to Zuki
Quite accustomed to ruling alone
As she wonders just why this intruder
Seeks invasion of her kingdom and home.

She spends hours sometimes in the watching
Contemplating who'll make the first move
Other times she just simply ignores him
Intimating there's naught here to prove.

It's a shame life for Ned's not exciting
When one thinks back to bushranging days
Poor Ned's reduced to rank boredom
And enduring domesticate ways.

His only diversion's my Zuki
When she feels like a change in her day
And she eyes him across the verandah
Daring Ned to get into his 'play'.

But life's brimful of disappointments
When Zuki's 'bout ready to pounce
She can see Neddy's legs seem to fail him
One more canine move to renounce.

So that's my iron watch dog called Neddy
Once included in shootouts and chase
Now reduced to a lifetime of leisure
And obediently glued in one place.

HI I'M ZURI

I cant work this humanoid out yet
Is she part of my family or wot?
I seem to've been passed on a few times
But is this my real mum or not?

My brothers and sisters departed
They left our snug nest one by one
Then I was scooped up and sent packing
Without being given the drum.

I should have twigged something was brewing
When I went through repairs in a fog
Like bubble bath manicure brushing
And deodorant specially made for a dog.

They put me in some sort of cage thing
I had darkness around for a while
It was scary I do have to tell you
And I cant say I travelled in style.

However I guess I could brag some
Not all dogs get to fly on a plane
But I have to admit that my 'snug' life
May not ever be quite the same.

Even my name has been altered
First Frosty then Zuffi -- oh gosh
I was just getting used to my callings
Now I'm Zuri - cant fathom this fuss?

What's in a name I say anyway
One seems to me good as another
I think it's to tie with the house name
Only humans would cause such a bother.

I noticed the sign read "Zuruka"
This dim puppie fast worked it out
Zu for Zuki who so sadly passed over
Mother Ruth – new sister Katrina no doubt.

Well my new mum I still cant yet fathom
I am getting my fair share of huggings
Inbetween this she spends her time shouting
And I think it's 'bout some of my doings.

Guess we'll have to play all this by ear now
And see who'll be first to give in
She thinks that I'm just a dim puppie
But I know in the end who will win!

ᴼᴼᴼ◯ᴼᴼᴼ

LIFE IS FULL OF SURPRISES........

One moment I'm strutting the 'dogwalk'
Posing and giving myself 'airs'
The next I'm leaping two at a time
On my way up my new mother's stairs.

It was really hard leaving my family
All my siblings and my own sweetest 'mum'
But the 'kids' were all off on endeavours
So I reckoned that my time had come.

It really all happened so quickly
E'en before I had time to say 'bone'
There I was being readied and crated
On my way to my designate home.

All my papers and stuff went before me
And arrived on the very same day
The stuff re my needles and anti's
So's my routine could go on the same way.

Of course all of my daily type schedules
Were passed deftly on o'er the 'phone
The foods that I liked or I didn't
Predesposing any reasons to moan.

I think my mum fast got the message
That I hail from a quite special line
Of beauty queens and so on etc.,
And of course I did give her the sign

By immediately casing surroundings
Then reclining on the best seat in the house
This left her to make do with leftovers
Which she did – quiet as a mouse.

I am learning each day re my mother
And as yet haven't formed a firm 'op'
She did seem to be a dead knockover
Now I see that she's not such a 'sop'.

She appears to be meekly agreeing
To all I put out as a test
Then she quietly manoeuvres around things
And ends up achieving her 'best'. (drat – woof.)

Well I guess I'm now pretty established
Have the run of the outside and in
Just so long as I stay within boundaries
Placed there by my mother's firm whim.

I'll keep you informed re my progress
As I secretly plan my next move
Life is certainly far from the humdrum
And there's always a challenge to prove.

But all said and done I must tell you
I am lounging in luxury plus
Lapping up all the good things around me
Special treats, hugs and kisses and fuss.

It feels good when my new little mother
Says "what a good dog you are Lexy dear"
And appeals to a spot deep inside me
That tells me I'll be real happy here.

PRINCESS LEXY

(a Lexy poem)

She is known as Princess Lexy
All around and up and down
She's as regal as any pup can truly be
When her silky plume she's flaunting
To the world she's upclass daunting
There's no doubt she's from a line of royalty.

Her proud stance, her toss of head
Her demeanour and her bearing
Every show of female form one cant deny
When out strolling in the park
She will leave a lingering mark
If she deigns to look your way while passing by.

Yes she hails from far horizons
Secret kingdoms, strange beliefs
In that mystic all mysterious magic place
Where the snowclad peaks on high
Pearce the clouds of heavens sky
And the awe of ancient rites breathes on your face.

You can almost hear the conches
And the radongs echoing sounds
Reverberating 'mongst the troughs and crags
See royal tibbies prayer wheel turning
Staunchly proudly Temple guarding
And the fluttering in the breezes of the praying flags.

It is plain our dearest princess
Has a background of aplomb
Filled with pride – ancestry shared by few
To this end we must kow tow
Present a reverential bow
Give our Lexy girl her inherent Royal 'due'.

A VENETIAN ALTERCATION
(A Lexy Poem.)

Oh despair, the moment's come
'You know what' has hit the fan
I thought 'twas too darn good to last
Right now I'm an 'also ran'.

My sweet new mum's quite out of tune
She's toned her voice way down
Instead of hugs and laughs and such
I'm faced with darkening frown.

It seems she noticed quite by chance
My latest alltime game
Of jump and catch and nip and snatch
Some beads I thought I'd tame.

These beads were getting on my nerves
When I felt bored one day
They, swaying, lashed right out at me
When my nose got in the way.

I was only checking stuff around
The way we young pups do
The door was open for the air
And the wind was blowing through

It rustled up the venetian blinds
'Till they rocked like an ocean wave
That's when I found myself attacked
And was forced my life to save.

I sprang at once into the fray
My good honour to defend
I chewed those beads that bind the blades
To a devastating end.

I must admit it felt real good
And victory won the day
'Till mother dear just happened by
And loudly had her say.

She was by no means very pleased
The blind blades floating free
And debris from my fight for life

For all and MUM to see.

I mean, you must remember after all
I hail from royal line
Accustomed thus to take the lead
And not myself confine.

If there's a thing that must be done
With snap decisions needed
I have to say that I'm right there
Solutions bravely heeded.

It's sad to be misunderstood
It makes my feelings jaded
What this poor pup has to endure
To see my mum persuaded.

Oh well I guess it wont be long
Mum and I'll again be friended
I heard her 'rranging on the 'phone
To have the Venetians mended. (sigh!)

WHEN THE 3 LITTLE PIGS
MET THE 3 BLIND MICE

The 3 little pigs went awalking one day
They'd partaken of quite a large lunch
And it helped their digestion down its easiest way
To prepare them to face their next 'munch'.

The forest was joyous at this time of year
It was Spring with all nature renewed
Birds whistled and sang skies were cloudlessly clear
All God's creatures with new hopes imbued.

Meanwhile further on down in a neat hidey hole
The 3 blind mice were astir
To replenish their larder was their daily goal
Twitching noses confirmed the 'allclear'.

Off then they scampered on the known forest track
With keen whiskers like radar employed
Of a sudden their progress was slowed by a 'whack'
Caused by something they couldn't avoid.

They looked sightless about and they sniffed all around
Not knowing the why where or who
'Twas the 3 little pigs they'd unknowingly found
'cept so far they just hadn't a clue.

Their tiny hearts beat just like drums in their chests
What type of danger was here
With their thoughts in a whirl tried to reason at best
All the enemies they had to fear.

Then the 3 little pigs each with oink and with grunt
Said "okay then you midgets all's well
We're just out for a walk and not out to hunt
It's Springtime - Let Spring fever compel".

So they all walked together through the forest so green
And enjoyed all that Spring had to give
Birds, flowers, butterflies, all part of the scene
Sharing joy, friendship, love - that's to live.

CPSIA information can be obtained
at www.ICGtesting.com
Printed in the USA
BVHW071011010419
544230BV00005B/520/P